VICKI COBB'S
WHY DOES MY
ICE CREAM MELT?

Smart Answers to STEM Questions

To the memory of
Jason Schneider

Racehorse for Young Readers books may be purchased in bulk at special discounts for sales promotion, corporate gifts, fund-raising, or educational purposes. Special editions can also be created to specifications. For details, contact the Special Sales Department, Racehorse for Young Readers, 307 West 36th Street, 11th Floor, New York, NY 10018 or info@skyhorsepublishing.com.

Racehorse for Young Readers™ is a pending trademark of Skyhorse Publishing, Inc.®, a Delaware corporation.

Visit our website at www.skyhorsepublishing.com.

10 9 8 7 6 5 4 3 2 1

Library of Congress Cataloging-in-Publication Data is available on file.

Cover and interior illustrations by John Kurtz
Cover design by Daniel Brount

Print ISBN: 978-1-63158-345-2
Ebook ISBN: 978-1-63158-349-0

Printed in the United States of America

VICKI COBB'S
WHY DOES MY ICE CREAM MELT?

Smart Answers to STEM Questions

Illustrated by
JOHN KURTZ

R
FOR YOUNG READERS

NOTE TO ADULT READERS

This book is designed so that your child makes discoveries. It is inquiry-driven. Questions keep the child engaged. Children love to give answers and very young children are not afraid to guess incorrectly. Reading picture books aloud to children is also a very special activity because you share an experience together. There is lots of room for discussion around the questions and the observations. The activities are integrated into the reading, so there will be times when you stop reading and follow the directions in the book.

Most of the activities in the book involve observing and eating ice cream. Please have on hand the following supplies: well-frozen vanilla (or chocolate) ice cream, an ice cream scoop, teaspoons, tablespoons, ice cubes, a glass dish, a china cup, a paper cup, an insulated coffee mug (very important), a Styrofoam cup, and paper napkins or towels. Also, this book should be read inside where you have a freezer handy.

ICE CREAM SOUP

Ever eat ice cream soup? If not, here's how to make it. Put a scoop of ice cream in a dish.

Leave it alone. Wait. This is the slow but sure recipe for making ice cream soup.

THE SHAPE OF
FROZEN ICE CREAM

While you wait, look at the scoop of ice cream.
   Does it have a shape?
   Is it the same shape as the dish
or does it have its own shape?

If it is a scoop of ice cream, its shape is a hemisphere, which means "half a ball."

WHAT'S A SOLID?

Does the ice cream take up space? Things that have their own shape and take up space are called **solids**.

Frozen ice cream is a solid.

Do you see any other solids?

How about the dish? How about the table? How about a spoon?

FEEL HOW IT MELTS

Tired of waiting?

Put a spoonful of ice cream in your mouth.

Wait before you swallow.

Feel what's happening to the ice cream in your mouth.

Is it changing?

This change is called melting.

Let the ice cream melt completely in your mouth before you swallow it. It's a short wait.

Got that? Okay, now you can swallow.

Your mouth is the quickest and the best way to make ice cream soup.

WHAT MAKES IT MELT?

What makes ice cream melt? Here are some hints: Touch the ice cream. How does it feel?

Dry your finger.

Hold it in the air.

Is the air warmer or colder than the ice cream?

Put your finger in your mouth.

Is it warmer or colder than the air?

ONE WAY TO MAKE ICE CREAM MELT FASTER

Heat makes ice cream melt.

Heat is a kind of energy.

There is heat in the air and heat in your mouth.

Try to speed up making ice cream
soup in the dish.

HEAT AND MOTION

See what happens if you cut it up
in small pieces with your spoon.

When you break up the ice cream there is
more surface touching the heat in the air.

Next, try stirring the pieces around.

Stirring is motion energy that changes to heat.

Here's how you can prove that:

Rub your hands together quickly. See how they get warmer?

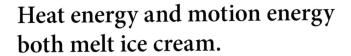

Heat energy and motion energy both melt ice cream.

When you have no more solid lumps, you've made ice cream soup.

WHAT IS A LIQUID?

Before you slurp your ice cream soup, pour a small amount into a paper cup.

It is now a liquid, so you can pour it.

Has it lost its shape?

All liquids, including ice cream soup, have the shape of the container and is flat where it meets the air.

Put the cup of ice cream soup back in the freezer.

Think you'll want to eat it after it's frozen again? You'll have to wait to find out.

It takes a few hours to freeze completely.

Maybe all day.

WHAT ARE THE PARTS OF ICE CREAM?

Ice cream is made of cream, milk, sugar, and flavoring like vanilla or chocolate. The part of ice cream that freezes is already a part of the cream and the milk.

Can you guess what it is? It is water.

ICE CREAM FACTORY

MILK

CREAM

THE ICE IN ICE CREAM

Know what you call frozen water?

Ice!

It's hard to see the ice in ice cream, so do what scientists do. They take apart their subject. They look at ice separately from ice cream.

Get an ice cube from the freezer. Touch it. How does it feel?

If you put it in a dish will it melt? You bet!

Scientists imagine how water changes from ice to liquid water.

First, imagine that water is made up of tiny particles that are so small that no one has ever seen them. They are called *molecules*. Water molecules are made of even smaller particles that stick together, called *atoms.*

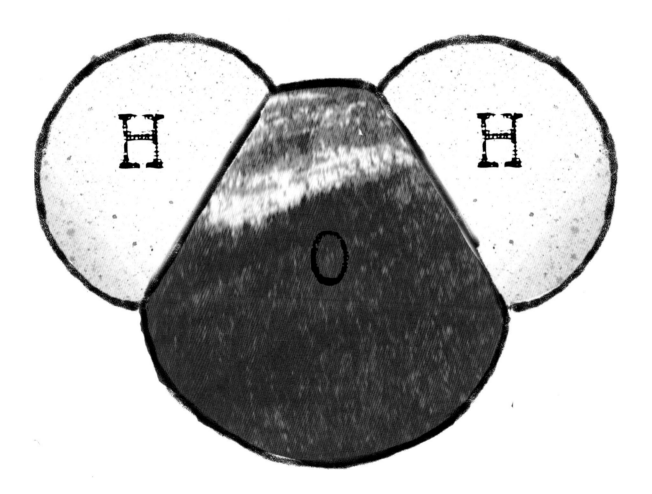

There are three atoms in a water molecule. Two are hydrogen and one is oxygen. We imagine that they are arranged like a face with two ears, almost like Mickey Mouse.

When water is frozen, the molecules are held together in a regular shape called a crystal. Snowflakes are tiny crystals.

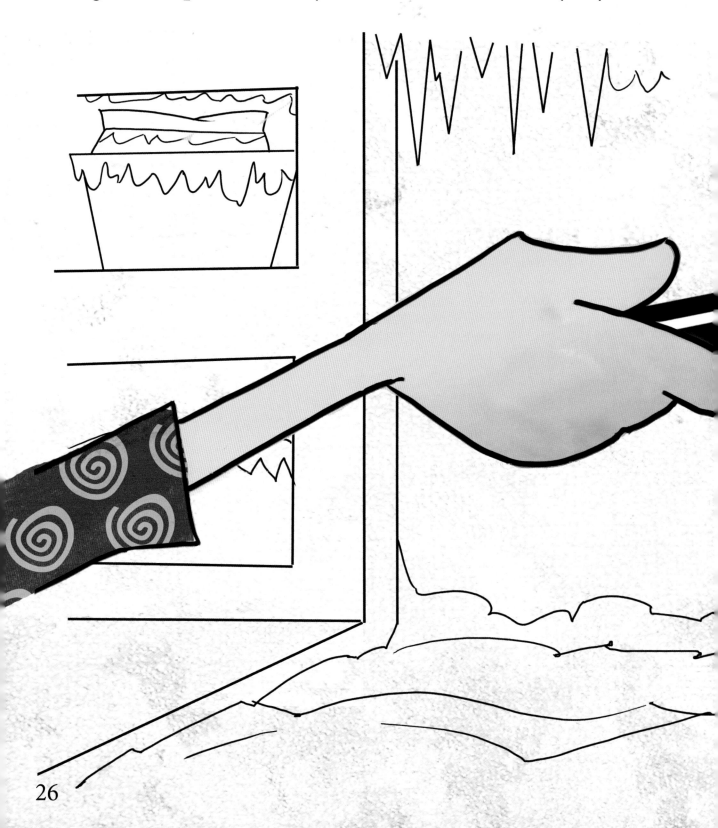

Look in your freezer; see
if you can find tiny ice
crystals. Those form
from water in the
air in the freezer.

Ice cubes are BIG crystals. In any ice crystal, water molecules can't move freely. They are in a regular shape that doesn't change.

The molecules can't move around, but they can shake in place. Heat makes them shake faster and faster until they become loose and can roll around each other.

That's what happens when they melt. In liquid water, the molecules are moving fast enough to roll over each other. They can stick together for a moment, but then break apart easily.

The space in the ice crystal is what makes ice float in real life.

IS THERE A WAY TO SLOW DOWN MELTING?

Do you like to eat solid ice cream better than soup?

Most people do.

So, here's the problem: Is there a way to keep your ice cream from melting too quickly?

That's the kind of question that is solved by scientists called engineers. What can you put it in so that melting slows down?

AN ICE CREAM MELTING RACE:
THE SET UP

Go on a container hunt in your kitchen.

Find small containers with bases that are about the same size. They should all be made of different materials. A dish, a china cup, a mug that is used to keep coffee hot in a car, a plastic cup made of styrofoam.

Line them up on the counter.

NOW FOR THE RACE

Working quickly, put a tablespoon of ice cream straight from the freezer into each container.

The Melting Race is on!

See how fast
they melt!

When the last one has melted, taste each ice cream soup.

Which is the warmest? Is one still cold?

HOW DO YOU SLOW DOWN MELTING?

The containers that keep things cold the longest are the coffee mug and plastic Styrofoam. That's because heat doesn't travel well through the mug or the Styrofoam. Materials that keep heat from moving where you don't want it are called insulators.

So, a mug that is designed to keep hot things hot, can also keep cold things cold.

You can experiment with other materials like foil or cardboard cups or ice cream cones.

Do they slow down the melting or do you just have to eat fast?

CAN YOU REFREEZE WATER?

See if the ice cream soup you put back in the freezer is frozen. You may have to wait until tomorrow to do this. If it is, try to stick a spoon in it.

Solid like a rock!

Try and taste it. Does it feel like there's sand in it? If so, the water has frozen into bigger crystals you can feel with your tongue.

That's because some of the water in the ice cream soup formed bigger ice crystals when you refroze them. It's not smooth like fresh ice cream.

Ice cream makers beat the ice cream as it freezes to keep the ice crystals so small you can't feel them.

WHAT YOU LEARNED AS A SCIENTIST AND ENGINEER

So now you know what makes your ice cream melt and why it melts. Remove heat and you get ice. Add heat and you get liquid water. Scientists discovered that the temperature of ice water doesn't start warming up until all the ice has melted. Scientists also discovered that the change is reversible. If you take out the heat from liquid water, it will freeze again. Engineers invented the ice cream maker. Engineers also invented the freezer, so now you can keep ice cream that won't turn into soup, and you can eat it whenever you like.

A BONUS EXPERIMENT

Here's another experiment that uses a scientific measuring instrument—a thermometer.

You will need a thermometer from your kitchen. Some thermometers measure in Fahrenheit units. On a Fahrenheit thermometer, the temperature of ice cream is 32° F. Other kitchens may have a Celsius thermometer. The temperature of ice cream is 0° C. Put a few ice cubes in a glass of water. Take the temperature of the ice water. Are they the same? Does the temperature change while the ice melts? Surprise! The ice water doesn't start to warm up until all the ice is melted. That's because the heat energy in the air and water is going into a changing the solid ice into a liquid. Once all the ice is melted, the mixture will start to warm up until it reaches the temperature of the air.

STEM WORDS
GLOSSARY

ATOMS: the smallest particles of all matter—solids, liquids and gases. They are so small, no one has ever seen one. We have to imagine what they are like. Some matter is made up of only one kind of atom. They are called elements. Hydrogen and oxygen are examples of two elements that are gases.

FREEZER: a closed container designed by engineers to remove heat so that it becomes cold enough to freeze water and keep it frozen.

FREEZING: the change from a liquid to a solid by lowering the temperature.

HEAT: a form of energy that is measured by temperature. It is produced by the motion of atoms and molecules, which we can't see but we can feel.

HEMISPHERE: a solid shape that is half of a solid ball.

HYDROGEN: the lightest element on earth. It is a gas which means it has no definite shape and it moves easily from one place to another. Two hydrogen atoms join with one oxygen atom to create water. A material that is made up of more than one kind of atom is called a compound.

ICE: water in its solid state. Liquid water changes to ice at 32° F or 0° C.

ICE CRYSTALS: when water freezes in ice crystals, the molecules are arranged like bricks, making a regular shape. You can see tiny ice crystals on the surface of foods in the freezer and by catching snowflakes.

INSULATORS: materials that absorb heat energy. Insulation in your house keeps the heat inside your house in the winter and keeps the building cool if you use air conditioning in the summer.

LIQUID: a material that flows from one place to another. It takes the shape of its container, but is flat where it meets the air. Water is Earth's most important liquid.

MELTING: the changing of a solid to a liquid when it is exposed to a source of heat.

MOTION: a form of energy that moving matter possesses. When you are running, you have more energy of motion than when you are sleeping. You are a big moving object. Molecules move faster the more they are heated. Their temperature increases, or the motion is used to change from a solid to a liquid.

OXYGEN: a gas in the atmosphere. It reacts with hydrogen to form the compound water. Water is our most important compound.

SOLID: a solid takes up space and has a definite shape of its own.

STYROFOAM: a plastic that contains tiny bubbles of air. It is a very good insulator. Styrofoam cups keep coffee hot and ice cream cold.

TEMPERATURE: the way we measure heat. The heat-measuring instrument is the thermometer ("thermo" means "heat" and "meter" means "to measure.") Temperature is measured in "degrees," which are the spaces between the lines on a thermometer. In the US we use a Fahrenheit scale, abbreviated as "F." The temperature at which water freezes is 32°F. Scientists and many other places in the world use the Celsius scale—abbreviated as "C." The temperature at which water freezes is 0° C.

WATER MOLECULES: are made of two atoms of hydrogen and one atom of oxygen. Chemists call it H_2O. It is a very stable molecule. You can freeze water molecules or melt them and there is no change in the molecule.

MORE VICKI COBB BOOKS
FROM RACEHORSE FOR YOUNG READERS